SO EASY HERBAL

SO EASY HERBAL

Ten Herbs:
how to grow them, use them, and save money

Karon H Grieve

Publisher's note
Every possible effort has been made to ensure that the information contained in this book is accurate, and the author cannot accept responsibility for any errors or omissions, however caused. No responsibility for loss or damage occasioned to any person acting, or refraining from action, as a result of the material in this publication, can be accepted by the author

First published in Great Britain in 2010 by Dream Acres
This edition published 2011 by Stenlake Publishing Ltd

Stenlake Publishing
54-58 Mill Square
Catrine
Ayrshire KA5 6RD
01290 551122
www.stenlake.co.uk

ISBN 978-1-84033-531-6

A CIP record for this book is available from the British Library

Visit Karon and Dream Acres on her daily blog at www.dreamacres.co

This book is dedicated to Idgy, my daughter, my friend

CONTENTS

ACKNOWLEDGEMENTS

I have to thank lots of people for helping me to bring all this together and make it come to life. So here goes.
Thanks to all those who told me 'You really should write a book' and then kept encouraging me when I doubted I could actually do it.
Thanks to the amazing Charlie Wilson for editing my words and making it all sound so much better, oh, and for correcting my dreadful spelling.
Thanks to Sharon Smith for pulling it all together and making it happen.
Huge thanks to my publisher Richard Stenlake of Stenlake Publishing Ltd for believing in my book bringing it to you.
Thanks to Janey Lee Grace for encouraging me and inspiring me, you are a star.
And biggest thanks of all to my family and friends for their unstinting support, especially to Idgy, my daughter, my friend, my helper, my inspiration and my Lavender Monster.

FOREWORD

At last, a simple guide to enjoying herbs! I confess to buying different herbs with grandiose ideas of infusing oils and cooking exotic delights, in reality I have mostly let them die off, or simply haven't been able to follow the complex recipes to use them to good effect.
Now I have no excuse! This is a back to basics guide to the top ten herbs, and how to use them to create all manner of goodies from teas and vinegars, to little sleep sacks.
I love the fact that Karon has made this accessible to all, even those without a garden can use a windowbox and benefit not only from saving money, but also patting themselves on the back for being resourceful and sustainable without a huge amount of effort.
Karon's passion for herbs really shines through in this very personal book, and if, like me, you've used her little sleep sacks (my four year old simply won't go to bed without it) you'll know that her simple ideas for using herbs in everyday life really work.
The perfect gift! A potted herb, or selection of seeds, and a copy of *So Easy Herbal – ten herbs: how to grow them, use them, and save money*. It should take over from candles and socks as the UK's favourite present for every occasion.

Janey Lee Grace
Author of *How to look good naturally – without ditching the lipstick, Imperfectly Natural Woman, Imperfectly Natural Mother and Toddler, Imperfectly Natural Home.*

Dear Karen,

HERBS AND ME

Here I sit in my garden in Ayrshire, pen in hand, listening to the gentle buzz of the bees and enjoying the fabulous fragrance of the herbs all around. This is me, this is my little corner of the world.

I love herbs. They are a big part of my life, and not just because I am writing about them here. I work with herbs and I use them in the kitchen and all over my home. They are just 'there', around and about in everything I do.

It wasn't always like this. I was a child of the sixties in small town Scotland, and we didn't see herbs much, other than the ubiquitous parsley as garnish on every restaurant plate whatever the meal. Herbs appeared for me in the seventies, on pizza and in 'foreign' food.

I remember hitch-hiking to Greece with my friend Alison when we were 17. We ended up in Delphi, a small village in the mountains and home of the most amazing ruins and the Oracle of Delphi. A village used to bus loads of visitors arriving in the morning and leaving *en masse* in the afternoon. We were something different: two teenage girls clutching Mary Stewart romantic novels and staying for a whole week.

We immersed ourselves in that village, in the books of the past and the romantic adventure of being away from home, adults on our own. We ate cheaply and well at the local tavernas and were introduced to herbs with every mouthful we ate. Oregano, basil and bay, flavours we had only dreamed of and read of in the pages of a book, suddenly took shape and became real. For me, the herb had landed.

From then on I have always used herbs in cooking and had something growing to feed the pot, whether basil on the windowsill or parsley in the garden. Herbs were around; they were just there, quietly part of my everyday life.

Over the years I have been lucky enough to travel and work in Greece and her islands. I drank in the flavours of that country and my love of herbs expanded to fill a whole garden when I returned to live back home in Scotland.

For me, herbs were firmly placed in the kitchen. It wasn't until the 1990s that I really thought about herbs in any other way. I had to give up the sculpting I had been doing for years due to severe nerve damage in my wrists, and I had to find something else to do. I'd worked for myself for years and I wanted to continue doing so; I just had to find some other way of doing it.

Enter the herb in all its glory. I was pottering in the garden when I thought about using my herbs in ways other than in the kitchen. My thoughts went back to my childhood and I placed herbs outside the kitchen, some snippet of memory I had stored away but completely forgotten. My grannie used to make little herb bags that she called 'taggies' to hang in her wardrobe to keep the dreaded moths at bay. I couldn't remember what she put in her taggies, so asked my mum.

She remembered lavender, thyme and rosemary. I went online to discover what I could about herb scenters and their uses. I discovered another world, a world of fragrance and creativity where herbs were used in so many different ways. From medicine to cleaning, air freshening to sleep, moth-chasing to flavouring, herbs do it all.

I bought books and more books, I trawled the internet and I learned all I could. I discovered that my love of herbs had extended from the kitchen and spread all over. The more I learned, the more I wanted to know. So what did I do with all this herbal knowledge? I enjoyed it, I revelled in it and I made it my own. I mixed it up with other things I loved – sewing, vintage fabrics and making things.

The first things I crafted with my herbs were footsees, little boot shapes made from old French fabric and stuffed with a tangy freshening blend that really made even the worst wellies smell great. I made sleep sacks too, using gentle chamomile, lavender and lemon balm. I gave these little goodies away to friends and family and found that they loved them too. From my little garden in Ayrshire and my kitchen table a new business was born, Dream Acres. Selling first at the village summer fete, I was soon a regular at the big Country Living and other mainstream fairs. Dream Acres goodies were featured on television and in a wide variety of magazines both here and abroad. They were sold in shops far and wide and I was always busy either gardening or sewing.

ONJOUR

So many people asked how I made things, what herbs I used and how I did this and that. The thought of a book was at the back of my mind but it was a big, scary idea, something I just didn't think I could possibly do. There are so many books out there: books on gardening, books on cooking, books on crafting. There are books on herbs that tell you how to craft and cook as well as grow these fabulous little plants. With so many books, could I possibly have anything more to add?

But what I couldn't find out there in the mega market place was a book that narrowed the field; a book that took just a few herbs and showed you just how fabulous those herbs were and how useful they could be in your day-to-day living; a simple book that took you from the garden centre to the kitchen table, whether you were cooking or crafting.

So that is where the idea for *So Easy Herbal* came from. I chose the top ten herbs that you can find at any garden centre; herbs that are not expensive or difficult to deal with in any way; herbs you can grow in a windowbox, patio planters or in a garden patch, however small. I wanted to let you see just how great these plants are and to hand you a smidgen of the enjoyment I have taken from growing and using my own herbs in so many different ways. So here it is, *So Easy Herbal.* I hope you will enjoy reading it and learning as much as I have.

Karon H Grieve
Dream Acres
Scotland
June 2010

HERB SPEAK

Let's keep things simple right from the start. You don't need to read through acres of text to deal with herbs. There are just a few words that you need to know as you'll see them on plant labels and in any descriptions of herbs.

Annuals: These plants do everything at once. They grow from seeds to maturity and then die all in one season. These are the herbs you put in new every season.

Biennials: They live for two seasons; germinating and forming leaves in their first year, and flowering, creating seeds and dying in the next.

Perennials: These plants live for at least three seasons and die back in winter and re-sprout from the roots in spring, or are woody like trees. Having said that, hard winter frosts can kill these guys off even when they are in their dormant stage.

Evergreen: The name says it all – these plants keep their foliage all year round. Great for keeping life around you when everything else has either died off or gone into winter sleep.

Tender: They really don't do cold at all. I know how they feel.

Hardy: Can take more chill but not frost.

That's it.

MENU FOR SUCCESS

There are only three basic things to remember with your new herb garden. These three things are all important and basically are the menu for herbal success.

Water

Herbs are not big drinkers, but they must be kept moist in the summer months.

Sunlight

Like us herbs like to feel the sun on their faces, so make sure you place them in their most favoured position.

Drainage

Our herbs are all from the Mediterranean and don't like to have their feet wet, so make sure there are drainage holes in your pots and containers.

If you follow this menu, your herbs should thrive and show their appreciation by supplying you with a fabulous bounty all summer long.

DIGGING THE DIRT

When I get started on something new I want it to be 'there' right away. I don't want to have to wait for seeds to germinate and things to sprout. Call it laziness and lack of patience if you will, but I prefer to think of it as an urgent enthusiasm!

So let's head for the garden centre and get started on your new herb garden right away.

Select bright and healthy looking plants. Resist the temptation to go for any reduced price 'has beens'. You want something that gives you a good start, not ongoing hassle and no return for your money.

While you are in the garden centre invest in a sack of growing compost and some fine gravel. You will need this to fill the new containers for your plants.

Ensure everything is well moistened when you prepare your containers and place your herbs either individually for single pots or as part of mixed groups, or in groups of three for a good solid clump.

Groups should be 8 inches apart for maximum growth. I know it looks sparse to start with, but believe me, your little darlings will soon fill out.

Buy 2
for
£5
£2.98
each
Save 96p

CONTAIN YOURSELF

The herbs we are using here are all well suited to container growing; in fact, I prefer having them in pots, pans and baskets so that I can move them about for best sunlight and to create different settings with them.

Be creative with your containers. Terracotta is always a favourite but it is expensive and heavy, heats up in summer and is apt to crack in winter. Plastic pretending to be terracotta is lighter and lasts longer, but doesn't really look as good as the real thing. However, you can always give it an aged and more realistic look by coating it with plain yogurt and rubbing on a bit of moss. It will soon take on that 'old garden pot' look if you leave it outside for a few weeks.

Why not 'think outside the pot'? Look at baskets, old buckets, bread bins, olive oil cans, soup cans, watering cans, fruit boxes and even wellie boots.

Just bear one thing in mind: drainage. Make sure you put holes in the base so that your herbs never get waterlogged. Remember: herbs hate wet feet!

YOUR TOP TEN HERBS

Basil

Chamomile

Lavender

Lemon balm

Marjoram

Parsley

Peppermint

Rosemary

Sage

Thyme

BASIL
PLACE A POT OF BASIL ON KITCHEN TABLE
OR AT THE WINDOW TO KEEP FLIES AWAY
HEALTH
CRUSH FRESH BASIL LEAVES INTO HONEY AND TAKE A SPOONFULL WHEN A NASTY COLD STRIKES
Simple Pesto
Basil
Parmesan
Pine nuts
Garlic
Olive oil
GOOD WISHES
Language of flowers.
KEEP THAT SUPERMARKET BASIL FAR LONGER BY PLUCKING OUT HALF THE STALKS AT THE ROOTS
MORE SPACE MORE LIFE!
BASIL (Ocimum basilicum)
Tender annual with oval shaped leaves and clusters of small white flowers in summer. 20-45cm Likes rich damp soiland full sun. Uplifting and refreshing aroma which aids concentration. Great spicy addition to salads.
BASIL IS TH "KINGLY HERB"

CHAMOMILE
PATIENCE
Language of flowers
PLANT ROMAN AND GERMAN VARIETIES.
KEEP PICKING THE FLOWERS.
THE MORE YOU PICK, THE MORE YOU GET
HONEY
Use a clear honey and heat in non metalic pot with 2tbs of Chamomile flowers. Simmer 20 minutes. Cool and strain into jars. Use on scones and sandwiches to tempt Bears on Picnics!
GROW CHAMOMILE IN A BEDROOM WINDOW BOX. THE SUMMER BREEZE WILL WAFT THE SLEEPY SCENTS INTO YOUR ROOM AND HELP TO LEAD YOU TO THE GENTLE LAND OF NOD
ZZZ
CHAMOMILE (Chamaemelum nobile)
Hardy evergreen, 20-30cm. Fluffy narrow leaves with daisy like flowers in summer. Likes full Sun and Light well drained soil. Has a gentle soothing fragrance that aids sleep, the sweet appley taste makes great tea.
Use as a rinse for golden Hair.

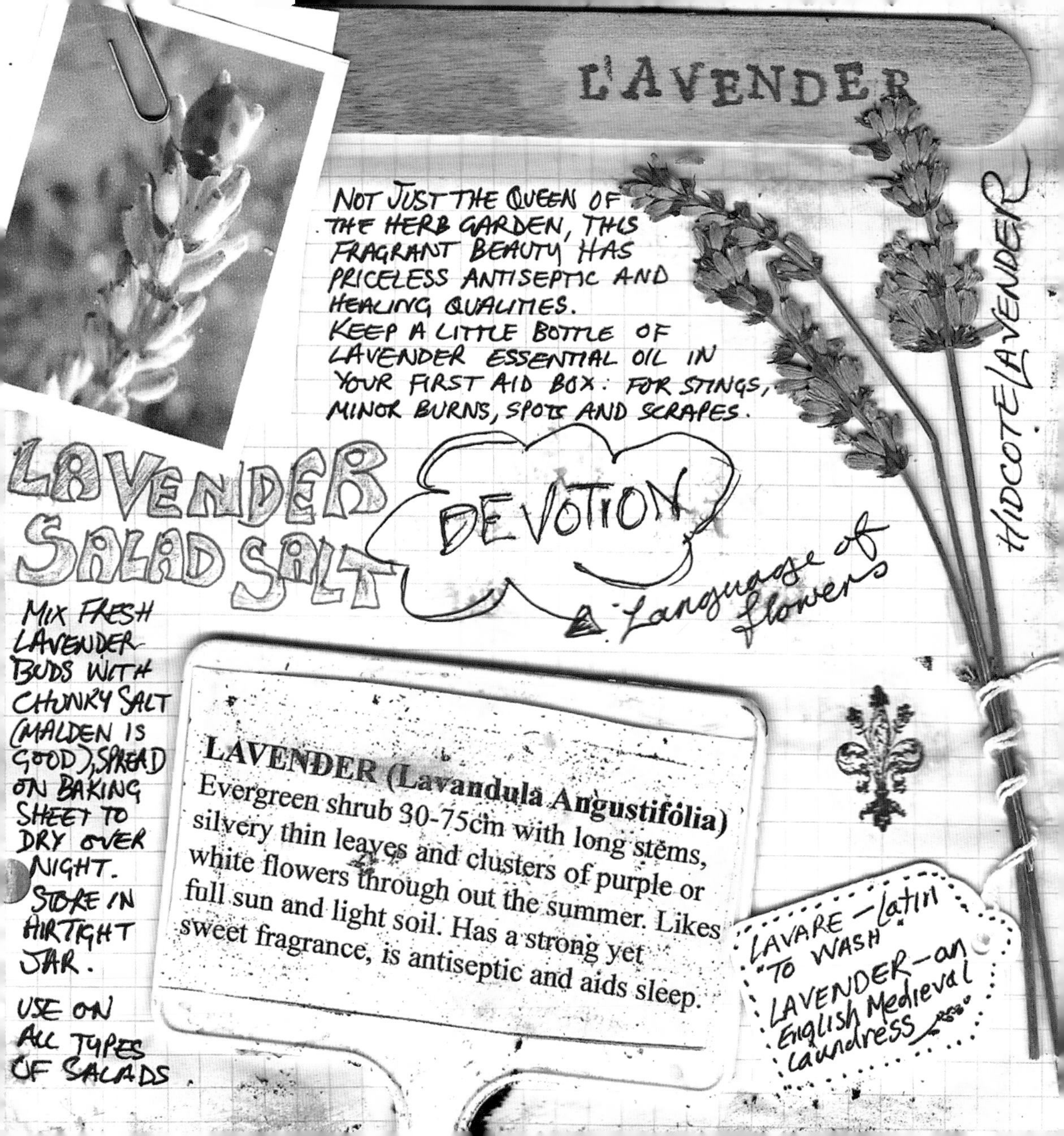
L'AVENDER
NOT JUST THE QUEEN OF THE HERB GARDEN, THIS FRAGRANT BEAUTY HAS PRICELESS ANTISEPTIC AND HEALING QUALITIES.
KEEP A LITTLE BOTTLE OF LAVENDER ESSENTIAL OIL IN YOUR FIRST AID BOX: FOR STINGS, MINOR BURNS, SPOTS AND SCRAPES.
HIDCOTE LAVENDER
LAVENDER SALAD SALT
DEVOTION
Language of flowers
MIX FRESH LAVENDER BUDS WITH CHUNKY SALT (MALDEN IS GOOD), SPREAD ON BAKING SHEET TO DRY OVER NIGHT.
STORE IN AIRTIGHT JAR.
USE ON ALL TYPES OF SALADS
LAVENDER (Lavandula Angustifolia)
Evergreen shrub 30-75cm with long stems, silvery thin leaves and clusters of purple or white flowers through out the summer. Likes full sun and light soil. Has a strong yet sweet fragrance, is antiseptic and aids sleep.
LAVARE — latin "TO WASH"
LAVENDER — an English Medieval laundress

L'EMON BALM
THE ANCIENT GREEKS AND ROMANS USED IT TO STAUNCH BLOOD IN WAR WOUNDS.
IN MIDDLE AGES IT WAS PLANTED BY DOORWAYS, TO WARD OFF EVIL SPIRITS.
IT IS THOUGHT TO BE A LOVE CHARM TOO
Melissa is Greek for Bee
They lov
it
SUN TEA
FILL A JAR WITH LEAVES & TOP WITH WATER. COVER AND LEAVE IN SUN ALL DAY.
STRAIN AND SWEETEN WITH HONEY.
SERVE OVER ICE FOR A TASTE OF SUN SHINE.
SYMPATHY
Language
flowers
LEMON BALM (Melissa Officinalis)
Bushy perennial 1m tall with nettle-like rough textured leaves and pale yellow flowers in late summer. Not fussy, grows in almost any soil and in sun or partial shade. Has an uplifting minty lemon smell and great lemony taste.

MARJORAM
A GREAT ANTISEPTIC
THAT LIFTS THE
SPIRITS TOO.
PART OF THE
OREGANO FAMILY
MEANING
MOUNTAIN JOY
MOTHS
HATE
IT
MARJORAM WITH EGGS
AND CHICKEN TOO!
JOY
Language
of
flowers
MARJORAM (Oreganum Majorana)
Hardy perennial 15-30cm oval leaves and
small pinkish white flowers in summer.
Likes full sun and well drained soil. Closely
related to Oregano, it has a sweet warming
taste and a gentle scent.

PARSLEY
PARSLEY CONTAINS MORE VITAMIN C THAN AN ORANGE. IT'S GOOD FOR YOU.
BREATH FRESH
Language of flowers
MERRIMENT
THE ROMANS WORE GARLANDS OF PARSLEY TO WARD OFF INTOXICATION
HIC!
PARSLEY (Petroselinum)
Hardy biennial 25-45cm. Flat leaf or curly varieties. Likes sun or some shade and a moist rich soil. Flat leaf has more flavour than the curly type. Both are good for the digestion and great breath fresheners too

PEPPER MINT
THERE ARE A MULTITUDE OF MINTS.
ALWAYS
CONTAIN YOUR MINT OR IT WILL TURN INTO A MONSTER!
FIRST AID
Rub on insect stings to ease pain
Make a strong mint tea & pour into foot bath with Epsom Salts to ease tired & swollen feet.
Mint tea for tummy upsets.
MICE HATE MINT
WARMTH
language of flowers
PEPPERMINT (Mentha Peperita)
Hardy perennial 4-100cm with prolific bushy growth with small white flowers in summer. Not fussy, likes sun or shade, and rich damp soil. There are many different types of mint, this is one of the most popular. Has a refreshing, cooling scent and strong taste.

ROSEMARY
PLANT NEXT TO CARROTS TO KEEP CARROT FLY AWAY.
ROSEMARY IS SOMETIMES KNOWN AS THE CHRISTMAS HERB. IT IS SAID THAT ROSEMARY RECEIVED HER BEAUTIFUL BLUE FLOWERS WHEN MARY THREW HER CLOAK OVER A BUSH WHICE THE HOLY FAMILY FLED INTO EGYPT.
FIRST AID
Gently massage Rosemary oil into temples to releive a headache.
REMEMBRANCE
Language of flowers
DEW OF THE SEA
ROSEMARY (Rosmarinus Officinalis)
Hardy evergreen shrub 30cm-150cm. Needle like leaves and blue or white flowers in Spring and sometimes Autumn. Likes sun and well drained soil. Strong and invigorating scent, great flavour and antiseptic too.
Great rinse for dark hair

SAGE

ROSEMARY
+
SAGE
PLANT THEM NEXT TO EACHOTHER AND THEY BOTH IMPROVE FLAVOUR

FIRST AID
A GREAT GARGLE FOR SORE THROAT.

WISDOM
→ Language of Flowers.

TAKES IT'S NAME FROM LATIN "SALVEO" → TO HEAL.

Sage cuts fat in cooking. Perfect for Goose sausages and Pork.
→ STRONG FLAVOURING.

SAGE (Salvia Officinalis)
Hardy evergreen perennial 30-75cm. Long oval shaped velvety leaves. Likes sun and well drained soil. A strong stimulating almost dry aroma and a really strong flavour that balances fatty meats when cooking.

THYME
THYME
Thyme is perfect with mushrooms.
Salads, stews, soups and fish are all fans of thyme
No kitchen should be without it.
ROMAN SOLDIERS BATHED IN THYME BEFORE GOING INTO BATTLE, TO GIVE THEM COURAGE.
COURAGE
language of flowers
A LITTLE LEAF, A LOT OF FLAVOUR
THYME (Thymus Vulgaris)
Hardy evergreen perennial 4-30cm with tiny leaves and miniature mauve or white flowers throughout summer. Sunny position and well drained gritty soil. A real taste of the Mediterranean with a stimulating scent.
THYME IS OF THE ESSENCE
NEVER ENOUGH THYME

So there you have it, our top ten herbs.

Now let's get started and have some fun!

THE HAPPY HARVESTER

Harvesting your little herb crop should be a pleasure, not a chore. You have planted these little beauties, fed them and cared for them, and now is the time to reap the rewards.

When: Often, the more you cut, the more you get! Always harvest on a dry day, mid morning when dew has dried but before midday when the sun will dry out those precious essential oils.

How: Use small sharp scissors or a gardener's knife and only cut the top third of the plant. You want to leave plenty of healthy body for more growth throughout the season.

Applemint
Rosemary
Thank

HOME AND DRY

Drying herbs is a very traditional way to preserve them for future use.

After cutting your herbs gather them in small bunches. Keep these small, about ten sprigs each.

Secure the bunch with a rubber band – a great use for all those bands that you get with your mail and better than string because herbs shrink as they dry and this way you won't have a floor littered with bits.

Hang your bunches with space between each in a well-ventilated area. To keep their colour, hang them in a shaded area out of direct sunlight.

It usually takes about a week for your herbs to dry completely so that they crumble easily when pressed between your fingers.

To speed things up you can dry them in the oven. Use at the lowest setting and spread herbs on a baking tray in a single layer. Check them every ten minutes.

Some people use their microwave to dry herbs; personally I do not recommend this as the microwave tends to burn out those precious essential oils that make herbs so special.

THE BIG CHILL

You can also go the opposite route in preserving and freeze your produce. This is a very good method for future cooking projects and means you have the herbs close to hand in the freezer.

Bag it: The first and easiest is simply to pop the cut herbs into a freezer bag, label and seal.

Oil method: Chop finely and place into ice cube trays, then top up with olive oil. The oil will never fully set so always keep the tray level in freezer. Great for soups, stews and pasta dishes.

Water way: Chop finely and put in ice cube trays topped with water. When frozen decant into a freezer bag, label and use as before. This is also good for iced teas and drinks like Bloody Marys or Mojitos.

HEINZ
Cream of
Tomato
soup
with
a hint of basil

COOK'S TOUR

It was Greek food that first really introduced me to herbs; those rich stews, fresh salads and fish dishes all packed with the magic of herbs. Many people think of herbs and cooking in terms of those dusty little jars that you remember to dig out from the back of the cupboard once or twice a year. These really do give herbs a bad name; forget them and either use herbs fresh or dry your own for use all year round. You will really notice the difference. By the way, dried herbs tend to lose their flavour after a year, so toss them out and renew your supply.

I love cooking with herbs. I adore the way that they can change the simplest dish into something truly awesome. You need not be Jamie Oliver or Heston Blumenthal to create magic with herbs in cookery. You just need to add a pinch here and a dash there.

'But I don't know what goes with what' is often the cry. Well, next I'll give you a simple list of what works for me in the pairing game. Use this as a starting point and try your own variations too.

This isn't a cookbook, so I'm not going to go into pages and pages of detailed recipes. Instead I'm giving you the 'how to' on herb-infused oils, vinegars, dried blends, butters and sugars that you can keep in the pantry and freezer and use to add excitement and flavour to your own dishes all year round.

All my projects are simple to make and you'll find they are great time-savers in the kitchen too.

PERFECT PARTNERS

Here are some ideas of partnerships between our ten herbs and their foody friends. Don't just limit yourself to these options. Use them as a starting point for experimentation. After all, taste is just that: a matter of taste, your own personal taste.

Beans	Thyme
Beef	Rosemary, marjoram
Bread	Marjoram, sage, thyme
Cakes	Lavender, lemon balm
Chicken	Marjoram, mint, sage, rosemary
Eggs	Marjoram
Fish	Basil, mint, parsley, thyme, rosemary
Fruit salad	Mint, lemon balm, lavender
Ice cream	Lavender, mint
Potatoes, boiled	Mint, parsley
Potatoes, roasted	Thyme, rosemary
Rice	Parsley
Soup	Marjoram, parsley
Stew	Marjoram, parsley, thyme
Tofu and Quorn	Sage, rosemary
Tomatoes	Basil, thyme, rosemary, marjoram, parsley

HERB OILS

Everyone uses cooking oils of one kind or another, but have you thought of making your own herb-infused oils that will not only enhance the food you cook, but make things that much quicker in the kitchen?

The easiest way to make a herb oil is to lightly bruise your herbs (approx 1 cup of herbs to 2 cups of oil) and put them into a wide mouthed jar (Kilner jars are excellent for this), add your oil (olive or vegetable) and give it a good shake. Place in a dark cupboard for at least a week to let flavours develop, then strain out herbs and decant into a nice bottle.
Try these:

Parsley and sage: A classic for salads, poultry and fish.

Marjoram: A good salad dressing, especially on tomatoes.

Lemon balm: Light and lemony flavour, perfect for drizzling on summer salads and fish dishes.

Basil: Has a slightly peppery tone which goes very well with many Mediterranean dishes. Add a dash of chilli for Asian cuisine.

Rosemary: Has a strength and flavour all of its own. I use this one for robust cooking, especially in winter. It is also wonderful on tomatoes.

Thyme: Works well with lemon and makes a very useful tangy oil and a good all-round kitchen standby.

100% RECYCLED

HERB VINEGARS

If the word vinegar just brings to mind fish and chips, then think again. Herb vinegars are a delight to the taste buds and a real benefit to your store cupboard. The easiest way to make them is as follows:

Take your selected herbs and bruise lightly to release their oils. You will want approx 1 cup of herbs to 2 cups of vinegar. Put your herbs into a wide mouthed jar (Kilners are a good choice) and pour in the white wine vinegar. Give it a shake and pop into a dark cupboard for a week giving it a shake now and then. Test for strength, strain out herbs and decant into a pretty bottle.

Here are some good flavour combinations:

Thyme and sage: A strong vinegar ideal for dressings.

Mint: Perfect for fruit salads or a simple green salad or a dash in apple juice.

Mint and rosemary: Perfection with lamb.

Basil: Add to tomato salads and a Bloody Mary.

Lemon balm: Great for fruity drinks; pineapple juice works well.

Mixed herbs (basil, marjoram, rosemary and thyme): A good all-around vinegar.

HERB BLENDS

Create your own special dried blends to add extra flavour to your soups, stews, pizzas and wintery salads.

You can also use these to mix with cream cheese for a good spread for crackers. Leave this in the fridge overnight for the herbs to flavour the cheese properly.

Mix with mayonnaise and plain yogurt to make a great dip for *crudités* and crisps, or flavour breadcrumbs for fish, chicken and pork by mixing the dried blend with fresh breadcrumbs.

Here are a few of my favourite blends:

Italiano
2 parts each of basil, parsley and marjoram
1 part each of thyme and rosemary
Dash of dried garlic

French fancy
2 parts each of rosemary, marjoram and thyme
1 part of lavender

Country garden
2 parts parsley
1 part each of sage, rosemary and thyme

HERB BUTTERS

This is something I always keep on hand in the freezer. It is just one of those little time-saving ideas that really is so simple and just so damn smart. You can use either dried or fresh herbs for this. Just remember that dried herbs are twice as strong as their fresh counterparts, so use half the amount.

250g unsalted butter
4 tbsp chopped fresh herbs
or 2 tbsp dried herbs
1 tbsp fresh lemon juice
(use a blender for a really fine mix)

Mash the butter and blend in the herbs and lemon juice. Roll and wrap tightly in greaseproof paper. Keep in the freezer and slice when required. Use any of your herbs separately or together. Here are some ideas to try:

Rosemary and parsley butter: Excellent when pushed under the skin of chicken or turkey prior to roasting.

Basil butter: Fabulous on pasta dishes.

Mint butter: Makes cucumber sandwiches sing!

Add garlic or chilli for added interest.

SWEET NOTHINGS

Herb sugars, totally simple and simply super.

Few leaves of mint, lavender or lemon balm
1/2 cup caster sugar

Whizz in the blender until the herb and sugar are one. Store in an airtight container and use for extra flavouring in sweet dishes. Try these:

Mint sugar: Dip crisp green grapes in egg white and then frost with your mint sugar. Now pop them in the freezer and bring them out at the end of a meal. They are fresh, tangy and almost like a mini sorbet in your mouth – divine. Mint sugar is also good for adding to cocoa for a minty chocolate drink and it is fabulous on grapefruit for a breakfast treat.

Lavender sugar: Wonderful in simple biscuits – they have a taste all their own – or in cake recipes and scones too.

Lemon balm sugar: A great sweetener for tea, adding a zing to your cuppa.

Basil sugar: Works a treat on strawberries in summer.

CREAM DREAMS

Whipped cream with strawberries, or oozing from jammy scones and scrumptious cakes – delicious and delightful cream is the perfect accompaniment for so many sweet dishes. But why not add a dash of extra flavour with herbs and a little extra sweetness?
All you need is:

Whipping cream
Herbs of choice
Icing sugar

Bruise herbs by pressing on them with the back of a spoon to release their oils. Use the herbs sparingly as their flavour can be overpowering. Place in a bowl and pour over the cream. Cover and refrigerate overnight. Discard the herbs and whip the cream, adding icing sugar to taste. Try these:

Basil and orange: Use the rind of an orange with the basil.

Lemon balm: Fresh and tangy.

Lavender: For scones and shortbread.

Mint: A classic with strawberries.

Rosemary and amaretti: Follow the usual recipe but exchange crushed amaretti biscuits for sugar.

SIMPLY SALADS

Any self-respecting salad likes to be dressed up with a few herbs, but don't just stick to the tried and tested ideas, like always putting basil with tomatoes. Be daring – rosemary likes tomatoes too, you know.

There are so many variations on the salad theme. Here are a couple of my favourites to whet your appetite.

Minted cucumber salad

1 large cucumber
Small handful chopped fresh mint
Small handful chopped fresh flat-leaved parsley
Grated rind of 1 orange
100ml olive oil
100ml red wine vinegar
2 tbsp granulated sugar

Toss the cucumbers in a bowl with the mint, parsley and orange rind. Whisk oil, vinegar and sugar in a small bowl and pour over the cucumber mix. Cover and refrigerate for at least four hours or overnight. Toss again before serving on a bed of ice cold lettuce.

Summer thyme salad

3 large tomatoes
1 cucumber
6 spring onions
1 tsp fresh thyme
2 tsp mayonnaise
Salt and pepper to taste

Slice the tomatoes, cucumbers and spring onions. In a large bowl mix together all the ingredients. Cover and chill for at least two hours before serving either as a salad or as a sandwich filling.

Lemon balm pesto

Don't just stick to the standard basil pesto. Use your lemon balm to create this delightful pesto to serve with chicken or fish.

2 tbsp fresh lemon balm
50ml olive oil
3 cloves of garlic
2 tbsp pine nuts

Whizz everything in a food processor until you have the consistency you prefer.

JUST JELLIES

Mint jelly: Lamb, pork and ham

Thyme jelly: Good with beef or fish.

Lemon balm: A light tangy jelly, perfect for fish and poultry.

Basil jelly: Good with all manner of meals and lovely on bread.

Rosemary jelly: Good with lamb or beef.

Lavender jelly: Nice on scones.

Chamomile jelly: Has a wonderful honey flavour that tastes great on toast.

Sage: Great for turkey, chicken or pork.

Herb jelly:

900g cooking apples
Pared rind and juice of 1 lemon
Sugar
Large bunch of herbs

Wash and chop the apples, and place in a preserving pan with the herbs, lemon and enough water to cover. Bring to the boil and simmer covered for 30 minutes. Strain the mixture through a jelly bag/muslin overnight. Measure the juice and pour into the pan. For every 600ml of juice add 450g sugar. Stir over a gentle heat until sugar has dissolved, then boil rapidly for about ten minutes until the setting point has been reached. Skim and pour into warm clean sterilised and seal while hot.

2008
w/chicken

PARTY PIECES

Herbed cheese

Mozzarella, chopped
3 tbsp sunflower oil
1 tbsp fresh marjoram
4 tbsp fresh parsley
A few slices of onion

Combine herbs in a blender with onions and whizz. Put the herb blend, oil and mozzarella into a bowl and mix well. Cover and refrigerate overnight. Drain off oil and serve on crackers.

Rosemary skewers

Use long rosemary twigs as skewers for kebabs. Just take off the leaves (use to scatter on top of kebabs) leaving a tuft at the end, and push meat and veggies onto the stick. This not only looks good but flavours the meat too.

BBQ brush

Take long sprigs of rosemary, marjoram and thyme and tie them together tightly with natural twine to make a handle to hold. Pour olive oil into a jar and drop in the herb brush. Put on the lid and leave to soak for a few hours. Use this flavoursome brush to baste meats on the BBQ.

Lemon balm salsa

Mix chopped lemon balm with tomatoes, onion, garlic and chilli. Add good olive oil, a dash of sugar, and salt and pepper to taste.

MY TIME, TEA TIME

Herb teas, or tisanes as they are often called, have been around since the dawn of time and used in every civilisation for healing, religious ceremonies and, of course, pleasure.

I love tea. My mum always said I was a Tea Jenny, an old Scottish term for someone who loves a good brew. Until a few years ago it was always 'real' tea that I went for – none of that wishy washy herbal stuff for me; I liked my tea strong and flavoursome, a proper thirst-quenching, comforting cuppa.

Reading up on herbs so much, I really couldn't avoid all the information on herb teas and all the recipes for them. Were they any good? Were they that weak, insipid drink that I imagined? Time to give them a go.

So I did. I made teas of all sorts. I tried lots of different varieties and different styles. I tried the really basic single herb types, I blended different herbs together and I tried the herbs plus tea types. All are special in their own way and I'd like to share some with you.

MAKING TEA

Treat herb teas with a bit of respect: make them a treat, not a rushed cuppa that you hardly notice. Use a teapot or cafetière whenever possible. The mere fact that you are putting a lid on the pot means that those precious volatile oils will be kept in the pot and not just evaporate into thin air. Warm your pot first by swishing with hot water, now you are ready for the herbs.

Rough 'em up a little before you put them in the pot to make sure that fresh herbs are lightly crushed and dried are crumbled. This helps release the oils and makes for a tastier drink.

Use approximately one teaspoonful of dried herbs or two of fresh herbs per cup. When you are making herb teas of any sort always remember that dried herbs are twice as strong as their fresh friends, so one teaspoon of dried rosemary is the same strength as two teaspoons of fresh.

Water temperature is important – just at boiling point.

Leave your tea to infuse for eight to ten minutes. An old-fashioned tea-cosy will keep your pot warm so your tea is both hot and infused when you come to drink it.

Not sweet enough? Just add a little honey to sweeten the pot.

TEA BLENDS

Lavender's blue: A great blend to cheer you up.
1 tsp each of lavender, rosemary, lemon balm and mint

Head soother
1 tsp each of basil, chamomile and mint

Sleep tea: Let this lead you to the Land of Nod.
1 tsp each of lavender, chamomile and lemon balm

Tranquilitea: Calm those nerves.
1 tsp each of sage, rosemary and thyme

Cold comfort: Perfect for snuffles and sore throats.
1 tsp each of lavender, rosemary and thyme

Hot stuff: Cool a fever.
2 tsp sage
1 tsp peppermint

Morning after: Perfect for a hangover.
2 tsp thyme
1/2 tsp rosemary
1/2 tsp mint

COOL DRINKS

Lemon balm lemonade

4 unwaxed lemons
Bunch of lemon balm
125g sugar
150ml boiling water
600ml cold water

Peel the lemons and put the rind into a jug along with the lemon balm and sugar. Pour over the boiling water, stir well and set aside to infuse for 30 minutes. Squeeze the lemons and pour the juice into a large jug over ice. Add the lemon syrup and top up with the cold water. Decorate with a sprig or two of lemon balm.

Strawberry and lavender gin

400g ripe strawberries, sliced
175g caster sugar
750ml gin
8 lavender flower heads

Place everything in a jar, seal, keep in a cool place and shake every day for a week. Strain and decant into a pretty bottle. Serve over ice or with tonic. Sheer summer sunshine – wonderful!

WELCOME HOME

What got me into herbs was their use within the home. Okay, I loved using them for cooking, but it was their history within the home that really grabbed my attention and got me into the whole herb business.

I am a failed domestic goddess. Housework and I are not bestest friends. I do, however, like to use natural products wherever possible and make my own whenever I can.

Herbs have been used around the home since the dawn of time, from the Romans using lavender to freshen linens to the Middle Ages when herbs were strewn on every floor from cottage to castle, to keep fleas and infection at bay and to ward off 'ye evil airs'.

Herbs really reached their peak in Elizabethan times when the lady of the house would maintain a stillroom where she would gather her herbs and make liqueurs, scented pillows, candles, cosmetics and sleep pillows. Her recipes (or receipts, as they were then called) would be written down in a receipt book and this precious tome passed down from mother to daughter.

The Victorians were mad for herbs and made great use of them in fragrancing their homes. No parlour was complete without little sachets hanging from chair backs and bowls of pot-pourri on every available surface.

FRESH AIR

Air fresheners seem to get more outrageously fragranced every day. We are no longer content with what Mother Nature could provide; instead, we have weird combinations of exotic and imaginary scents being pumped from canisters that are actually polluting the air we are trying to fragrance and make 'natural' in the first place.
Enough, stop! Take a few minutes to make your own.

Air care spray
200ml water
Vodka, enough to cover the herbs
1/2 cup each of fresh lavender, rosemary and mint

Lightly bruise the herbs to release their oils and then push them into a wide-mouthed jar (a coffee jar is good). Pour in the vodka. Shake well and then leave to steep for two weeks. Strain and pour into a spray-topped bottle, and top up with water. Shake well before use, and do not spray directly onto your furniture.

Enjoy real fresh air.

HOME HELP

Remember Shake 'n' Vac? It's a powder you shake out onto the carpet and then vacuum up. The eighties advert had a catchy tune and showed a bright and cheerful housewife singing as she hoovered the floor and created a fabulous setting for her family and friends. Laughable though that is, you can be using your herbs in a similar way which harks back even further, to the Middle Ages.

Aroma rug

200g of dried lavender
100g dried rosemary
100g baking soda

Use a blender to really grind up the herbs, then mix all the ingredients well and store in an airtight container.
Just sprinkle this mixture onto rugs and carpets and leave for at least 20 minutes (for tip-top freshness leave overnight), then hoover up. The herbs will help keep bugs at bay and kill germs in the carpet, and your room will smell fabulously fresh too. This is really good if you have pets in the house.

Minty windows

My mum used to swear by vinegar for cleaning her windows, but I just swear when I have to clean mine. However, if you steep fresh mint in your white vinegar and then use that as a window spray, it works a treat and smells divine. Almost makes cleaning windows less of a chore . . .

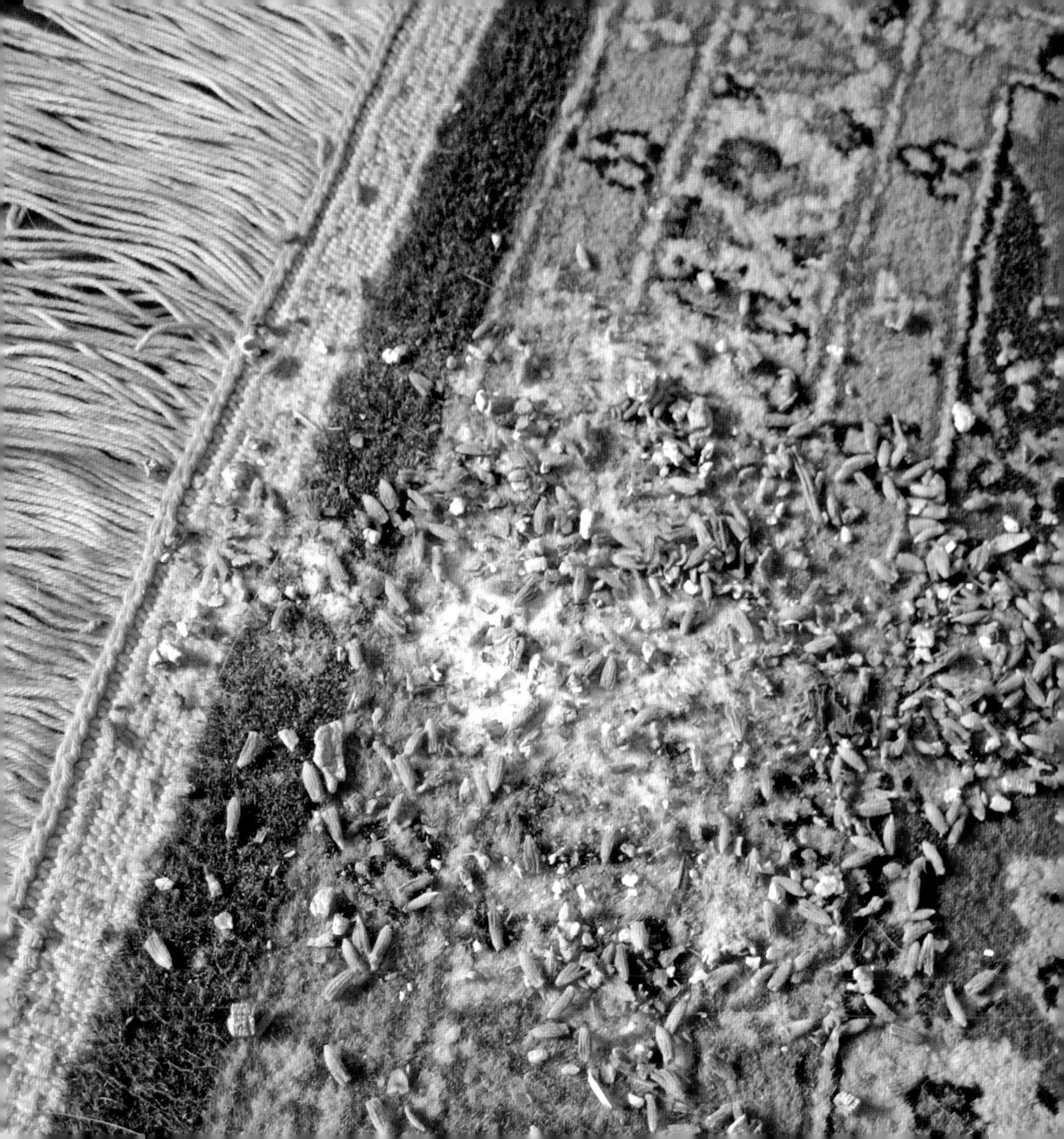

LINEN LOVE

This is my favourite part of herbing, and for me the most important part of herbs in the home. The mere thought of linen bags takes me right back to my grannie and sitting at the kitchen table as she delicately tied little bundles of cheesecloth filled with fragrant herbs to hang in her wardrobe and linen cupboard to keep moths at bay and make everything smell wonderful. They always say that smells are the strongest triggers to memory, and this is so true for me. Fragrant linen bags take me right back to being a little girl.

You can hang bunches of fresh lavender in wardrobes and linen cupboards and just let them dry out and work their magic on the moth population. This is fine, but you will end up with everything being covered in herb bits. It is always best to contain dried herbs for this job.

On the following page is my recipe for a great moth-chasing blend that uses some of our top ten herbs in their dried form. You can put the mix into anything that lets the fragrance out. For sheer simplicity (and no sewing at all), this could be an envelope with some pinholes and maybe a ribbon tied round it. Or make little bundles of herbs on a 6-inch square of fabric, gather up the sides and tie with a ribbon.

For those who want to sew, the sky is the limit. You can make fragrant sachets from any material and in any shape you like, from standard bags to delicate hearts, parcel-shaped pillows to complicated adornments featuring lace, beads and ribbons. It is entirely up to you. Whatever you choose, the moths will hate it.

Moth off

2 parts each of lavender and rosemary
1 part each of thyme, mint and marjoram
1 tsp Orris root powder
10 drops essential oil of choice

Mix the orris root powder with the oil and blend into your herb mixture. Store in an airtight glass jar for six weeks, shaking regularly. The orris root powder is not essential but does make your fragrance last longer.

You can add vermiculite or wheat to extend your mix and make it go further.

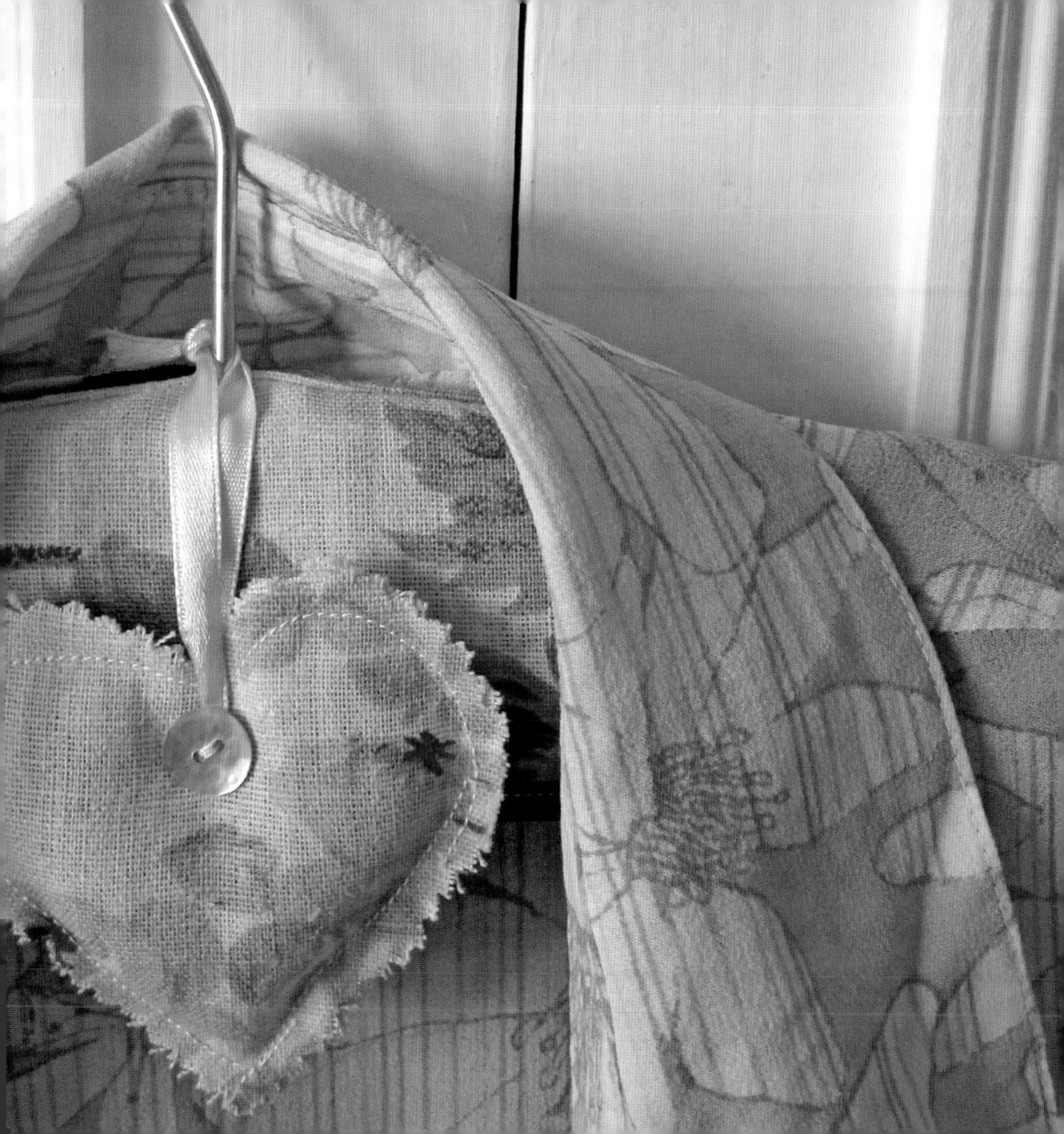

BATHING BEAUTY

Whether you are a relax-and-wallow-in-the-bath type of gal (like me) or one of those whose idea of heaven is a refreshing and invigorating shower, your herb garden can play an important part in your everyday bathing ritual.

Using herbs for bathing is hardly a new prospect. The Romans used lavender in their baths and the Ancient Greeks were fond of the odd sprig of thyme in the tub.

Fashions change, and although a great many bath and beauty products feature herbs in their make-up, it is surely far better to go completely natural and make your own bath goodies using the herbs themselves and not just 'fragranced with' varieties.

You don't need to have a degree in chemistry to make your own bath oils, bathing salts, soaps and tub teas. Just gather up your herbs and have a go.

For those who just don't have time for all this 'doing' stuff, you can always keep a selection of essential oils in the bathroom and just add a couple of drops to your bath and let the hot water do the rest. How simple is that?

A step further is to hang a bunch of herbs either to the tap (when using the bath) or from the shower head and let the rushing hot water release the essential oils of the herbs.

NEAR THE Sea
WE Forget TO
COUNT THE Days

SCENTY SOAP BALLS

These soaps make great additions to your bathroom and ideal gifts too. Just use dried herbs and unscented soap bars to make your own soap balls.

1/4 cup boiling water
1 tbsp dried herbs
5–6 drops matching essential oil
2 cups grated soap

Pour the water over the dried herbs. Steep for 15 minutes and add the essential oil. Reheat till bubbling and pour over the grated soap. Mix well with a wooden spoon and then shape into balls with your hands. Make them about the size of a golf ball. Polish the soap balls with a few drops of essential oil for a smooth finish. Set aside on greaseproof paper to dry out for three or four days.

Try these:

Chamomile: Good for delicate skins.
Sage: For oily skin.
Peppermint: Refreshing.
Rosemary: An astringent.
Lavender: Antiseptic and smells beautiful.
Thyme: Antiseptic and has a non-floral scent.

You can also add oatmeal for a beauty bar to soften the skin, honey – a great food for skin – and a Vitamin E capsule.

Add honey and ground almonds for an exfoliating gardeners' soap to scrub those hard-working hands. Lavender and rosemary are good herbs for this as they are both antiseptic and anti-inflammatory, so ideal for healing those scrapes and nicks.

BATHING SALTS

First things first, step away from the image that bathing salts are only for grannies at Christmas time. Bath salts have been used since Roman times for relieving aching muscles, improving the skin and as an aid to relaxation. Keep this in mind and banish all thoughts and images of lurid pink crystals in fake decanters with an aroma strong enough to revive a fainting elephant.

Our bathing salts are totally natural and bang up to date. They are also so simple to make, you'll wonder why you never got into them before.

200g Epsom salts
200g salt (big chunky stuff is great but any salt will do)
10 drops of your favourite oil, or make up a blend

Try these combinations:

Lavender, chamomile and lemon balm: Sleep easy.
Rosemary, peppermint and basil: Wake-up call.
Thyme: For aches and pains.
Lemon balm: Calming.
Basil and marjoram: For sore muscles.

BATH OILS

To make a simple bath oil use a light and inexpensive oil base like sunflower oil. I also add in the contents of a Vitamin E capsule to stop the oil becoming rancid over time; it also has great benefits for your skin.
All you have to do is pour the oil into a jam jar, pierce the Vitamin E capsule and add that, and then pop in your chosen herbs. Add a few drops of matching essential oils to give the mix extra strength. Leave this jar of goodness in a cupboard for two weeks and give it a shake now and then.
Now decant and strain into a pretty bottle and leave it ready by the bath. Just use about a tablespoonful in the hot running water, hop in, lie back and relax.
Try these:

Rosemary, marjoram and lavender: For aching muscles.
Rosemary, peppermint and lavender: A pick-me-up.
Chamomile, lavender and marjoram: Sleep dreams.

To create a massage oil use 60ml of almond oil as your carrier and a total of 15 drops of essential oils in your chosen blends. Please note, you must use a carrier oil as a base as essential oils are too strong to be used directly on your skin in this way.

TUB TEAS

If you don't want to use salts or oils in the bath then why not try these tub teas instead? Mix up your dried herbs (a handful will do fine) and put them either in a little muslin bag or in a tied-up hanky. Loose herbs floating around the tub may look very artistic, but the Ophelia look really isn't that great and you will arise like a swamp monster covered in greenery.

You can either toss the little bag into the bath as the taps are running, or for a stronger and more beneficial bath pour about 2 litres of water in a pot with your herb bag and boil it up, cover and simmer for ten minutes before emptying the lot into your bath – takes a wee bit more time but it's worth the effort.

Use your standard blends from the bathing salts page, like Sleep easy and Wake-up call.

For added skin softening and a bit of a beauty treatment, add half a cup of oatmeal to your tub tea blend. This has such a gentle smell and will make the water all cloudy and soft.

After you've wallowed enough, squeeze the bath bag and scrub over your skin to get the full benefit of the herbs.

HOME SCENTS

Pot-pourri comes from the French 'rot pot', which isn't really an auspicious start when you first think of home fragrance. Add to that the image of the usual shop-bought variety – bright pink curls of wood shavings, odd bits and pieces of unrecognisable nature and a synthetic chemical smell that leaves you with a headache and a house that smells rather like a public loo.

I have never been a fan of *pot-pourri*. In fact, it was one of those things that I just didn't fancy having around and certainly never wanted to make. It wasn't until my first Christmas running Dream Acres that I decided to give it a go and see if I could come up with something that I'd like to have in the house. I discovered that my simple herbs could be added to a few spices and other bits and pieces to create something really special and totally unique.

So it is time to shake off the outdated image of *pot-pourri* and embrace this ultimate 'green' air freshener for your home.

POT-POURRI

Herbs and spices for fragrance
Essential oils (10 drops of each)
1 tbsp orris root powder as a fixative
Bulking materials of choice (optional)

Place the orris root powder in a large ceramic or glass bowl. Add to each of your chosen oils and use a wooden spoon to blend really well. Now add in your herbs and any other goodies you fancy. Make sure everything is well mixed and pour into a sealed glass container. Let it mature for four weeks and then it is ready to use in open bowls.
Here are some blend ideas:

Lavender, peppermint and rosemary: For a bright fresh fragrance.
Lavender, chamomile and marjoram: A gentle fragrance, perfect for a bedroom.
Lavender, lemon balm and basil: A fresh and clean scent.

Good spices to use are cinnamon (which is a natural fixative), cloves and star anise. These will add a warmth and depth to your herbs.
Good additives to add bulk include pine cones, drift wood, corks, pebbles, sea glass, corrugated card pieces, dried grasses, nuts in their shells and broken pieces of unglazed pottery. Curls of citrus peel are great as they add their own fragrance and bulk too.

HOT STUFF

Simmering pot pourri

Very popular in America, naturally scented simmering pot-pourri is a quick and easy way of fragrancing your home via the kitchen.

Mix together a handful of dried herbs, any spices that you fancy and citrus peel of your choice. Toss all this into a pot containing one litre of water and bring it to the boil. Now, as the name suggests, let it simmer. The fragrant oils will be released by the hot water and your house will smell wonderful.

There is no need to use a fixative as you are using up the fragrance all at once while it is bubbling away on the stove.

Chafing

Chafing comes from the old French *chauffer*, "to make warm." It's a very old yet practical way to freshen your home.

Crush your herbs and spices and heat gently in a heavy based frying pan. When they begin to smoke, carry pan from room to room to freshen the air.

WAXING LYRICAL

Nowadays we rarely need to use candles as a necessary form of lighting. However, there is nothing like candlelight to add a touch of romance to a room. With just the strike of a match you can add magic and drama to any setting.

Fragrant and decorated candles are always popular but can be expensive. Make your own from simple plain white candles and some of your herbs.

Candles to decorate
2 dinner candles (for melting)
Finely crushed dried herbs
10 drops essential oil to match herbs

Melt the dinner candles using the double boiler method of one pot inside a larger one, with about 10 centimetres of water in the outer pot (never melt wax directly on the stove). Remove the wicks from the pot and add the essential oil. Set up a tray lined with baking parchment and scatter on this the herbs. Now carefully dip candles individually into the molten wax and then roll them on the herby tray. Dip again in the molten wax to seal in the herbs. Then set aside to dry thoroughly before use.

AND SO TO BED

Well, we have come to the end of my little herb book, and if you have read this far you should have picked up a bit of herb knowledge and hopefully a great big dollop of enthusiasm for these great plants and the things you can do with them.
Think of these ten herbs as your stepping stone, your first step in the exciting world of herbs.
I'd like to finish with my favourite herbal goody: my sleep sacks. These simple little sacks really launched Dream Acres in magazines and on television, and I must thank the lovely Janey Lee Grace for that.
Herbs have been used as a sleep aid for thousands of years. The Romans used to stuff mattresses with fragrant lavender, Tudor ladies would wear caps filled with lavender and Victorian ladies would blend herbs to make sleep pillows.

1 part each of lavender, lemon balm, chamomile and marjoram
plus a tiny dash of mint

Mix together the herbs then store in a sealed glass jar for six weeks to blend the scents together. Pop a spoonful into small bags, tied hankies, baby socks or even a pierced envelope. Leave by your pillow and sleep well . . .

SOURCES AND MEASUREMENTS

SOURCES

I have tried to use only easy-to-find ingredients throughout this book which you will find at any garden centre or plant nursery.
Always buy dried herbs, spices, essential oils and orris root powder from reputable suppliers.
Bristol Botanicals Ltd. www.bristolbotanicals.co.uk

MEASUREMENTS

All spoon measures are level.

¼ teaspoon	1.25ml
½ teaspoon	2.5ml
1 teaspoon	5ml
1 tablespoon (3 teaspoons)	15ml
¼ cup	65ml
1 cup	235ml
1 pint	600ml